# Benjamin Zephaniah

# TOO BLACK, TOO STRONG

D0993676

BLOODAXE BOOKS

Copyright © Benjamin Zephaniah 2001

ISBN: 1 85224 554 9

First published 2001 by
Bloodaxe Books Ltd,
Highgreen,
Tarset,
Northumberland NE48 1RP.


Bloodaxe Books Ltd acknowledges
the financial assistance of Northern Arts.

Cover printing by J. Thomson Colour Printers Ltd, Glasgow.

Printed in Great Britain by
Cromwell Press Ltd, Trowbridge, Wiltshire.

*For*
*Rada Gungaloo*

*A woman that works from the heart,*
*Because she loves and because she feels.*

*May all our women be free.*

# ACKNOWLEDGEMENTS

In February 2000 I started a residency at Tooks barristers' chambers in London. The residency was sponsored by The Poetry Society and although it was officially scheduled to run for 48 days I lost count of the days but spread my time there over a year. Poems in this book written during that period and inspired by the residency are: 'To Ricky Reel', 'To Michael Menser', 'Having a Word', 'Appeal Dismissed', 'Chant of a Homesick Nigga', 'I Neva Shot De Sheriff', 'Adultery', 'Two Dozen Babylon', 'Knowing Me', 'Derry Sunday', and 'The One Minutes Of Silence'. Other poems from that residency not included here were written for performance only. I would like to thank The Poetry Society for thinking up such an interesting residency and for putting up with my unorthodox approach to it, and everyone at Tooks who made me so welcome and managed to endure a year of me following them to court, questioning them, and loitering with intent. The administrators, the barristers, the clients, all helped to make my time with them the best term I have ever served.

With one or two exceptions the poems in this collection were written between the years 1997 and 2000. I have also included poems that started life as commissions: 'What If' was originally commissioned by BBC Television, 'What Stephen Lawrence Has Taught Us' by Independent Television News (ITN) for Channel Four News (and afterwards printed in *The Guardian*), 'Carnival Days' by The Post Office, 'The London Breed' by The Museum of London, and 'Heroes' is one of three poems commissioned by Sheffield City Council and carved into buildings in Rockingham Street in the centre of Sheffield.

Although you can find me on various Internet sites, there is one genuine Benjamin Zephaniah sites:
http://www.benjaminzephaniah.com

# CONTENTS

# WHAT AM I GOING ON ABOUT?

Britain is a wonderful place. It is a nation of shopkeepers, aristocrats, farmers and animal lovers, all at the same time. It has the "mother of all parliaments", its inhabitants enjoy "free speech" and the right to vote in open elections and it is so confident that it doesn't need a written constitution. Its cities are havens for the young; they pulsate to the music of the world, and though the skies may be grey for much of the year the streets are coloured by its people who now talk about "raving" just as much as they talk about the weather. The cities "rock". The same can be said for many of its towns; they may not have received the title of "city" from the Crown or be the "seat of a bishop", but they still have the attitude and the rhythm of the city. Above all the capital city shines magnificent through its pollution; it is amongst the heavyweights of cities: here it is estimated that over three hundred languages are spoken. But Britain is not just a collection of cities. The quaint beauty of the Lake District continues to inspire poets, and the grandeur of the Scottish mountains is famous all over the world. I have always admired the splendour of the Welsh Valleys; it seems to me this area represents both the picturesque and industrial side by side, for it is here that many of the nation's coalmines are to be found. In fact many of those coalmines were closed down in the 1980s and they have now become tourist attractions, and a chosen few coal miners who were once doomed to a life of unemployment are now paid to show you what they used to do. The same fate has fallen upon coalmines all over Britain. But Britain is not just a collection of unused coalmines or museums, what of British culture?

Well, to date, Britain has 21% of all major Oscars; 13% of television programmes shown at peak times worldwide are made in Britain; our pop music keeps conquering America; everyone knows of William Shakespeare and the Brontë Sisters, but what of the Teletubbies? Well they are one of the biggest single export products ever. All of the above represent an idea of Britain; we pick what we want to represent us depending on what type of "subject" we are. The title of British means many things to many people; some choose to remain forever nostalgic for its "days of former greatness" when Shakespeare was "Top of the Pops" and the sun never set on the empire, whilst for others it's about the melting pot, bursting with vitality and smiling multiculturalism. The latter will tell you that it is the great British Indian curry that binds us together; these people are out to carve out a new idea of Britishness and feel hindered by those whose only purpose is to preserve the past. We are all imagining Britain, but that's a luxury, what's the reality?

It is a place where African-Caribbean women make up 14% of the female prison population, whereas African-Caribbean people as a whole only make up 1.3% of the population of Britain. African-Caribbean and Asian people together make up 5.6% of country's population but 16% of the prison population. Anybody who knows anything about Britain knows that you are five times more likely to be stopped and searched by the police if you are African-Caribbean; it's also worth knowing that over 130,000 racist attacks happened in the year 2000. These figures weren't given to me by friends and family, these are official figures, government figures, the Commission for Racial Equality figures, and anybody who knows anything about official figures will also know they usually fall very short of the mark.

Many of us Brits are easily deceived; even I used to believe that the country was becoming overcrowded and the reason why so many Asians open corner-shops was that they didn't have the education to do anything else. The truth is that in the year 2000, 11,000 more people left Britain than entered, and over half of those given work permits were from the USA; and one out of every five Asian shopkeepers has a university degree: when asked almost every one of them said they opened up their own business because of racial discrimination by employers.

What refugees? From being totally uninhabited Britain has constantly taken in new visitors, be they Picts, Celts, Angles, Saxons, Chinese, Jamaicans, Jutes, Huguenots. All of them, with the possible exception of the Romans can be classed as refugees of one type or another. Some were fleeing religious persecution, others political persecution or racial persecution; some were even fleeing persecution from the weather, e.g. hurricanes and floods, but we all came here from somewhere. So in theory Britain should be the last place on earth where you should find racism. But the reality is that many people are suffering from what I call the 'last off the boat syndrome'. They conveniently forget their journey here and now live in the fear that Britain will be flooded by penniless asylum seekers who would then drain our precious society of everything they hold dear. The reality is that 30% of refugees have left professional jobs, 10% held managerial positions and only around 5% are unskilled. The reality is that refugees built the National Health Service, refugees built our roads, they clean our cars, and when given the chance new refugees contribute disproportionately to the economy because they have seen hardship and suffering and view economic success as a way of repaying their country of refuge.

Now let's go global. We live in a world where one in four people live in a state of absolute poverty; 35,000 children die each day because they are born to poor parents; each year 24,000 people are killed and maimed by landmines; and when you hear the information-rich telling you that the world is 'wired' and getting smaller, remember that most of the people on this planet have never even made a phone call. Do we communicate more? Well, the world stayed silent when the slave trade was making money; the world stayed silent when the Nazis started to kill trade unionists, disabled people, gays and Jews; and now, in the age of the global village and mass communication, the world is staying silent as the Palestinians are being annihilated. Countries are ostracised, isolated and starved of funds if they do not allow McDonalds to set up burger shops on their best spots on their best high streets, or if they do not allow the World Bank to dominate their poorest farmers.

Now this may not seem like the foreword of a collection of poems but it is important to me that the reader "overstands" the political landscape these poems are written in. I know that I risk being accused of being out of step with the current "artistic culture" prevalent in Britain today, but the thing is I don't have an identity crisis, and I have no wish to write to win awards. I am told that things could be easier for me if I "played the game" but I could never stand on a platform and honestly say that the height of my career was receiving an OBE, and in an environment where the artist is scorned for being political, I have to confess that I still believe that there are things that are more important than me or my poetry. We are allowed to shock, we can be outrageous, or if we want to act like we care we can do Band Aid, Live Aid and Comic Relief, but when we want to confront the dictators, the arms traders and deal with the "cause", we are confronted with a cut in our grants or a tearing-up of our contracts. For the time being the poet is no longer the 'unofficial legislator' (to use Shelley's phrase): that's the guy who makes the commercials; the art that sells is now the art of selling. Most people don't care what the product is, but it must be delivered in the right package; you are a member of a target audience. Yes I have let down those who believed that it would not be long before I sat down with them for endless sessions of intellectual masturbation. I just feel a sense of urgency and I may not be right but I feel that (my) poetry has a purpose, well many purposes.

These poems are about how I feel now. On one hand I think it my duty to travel the world for The British Council and other organisations, speaking my mind as I go, ranting, praising and criticising everything that makes me who I am, but this is what Britain can do. It is probably one of the only places that can take an angry, illiterate, uneducated, ex-hustler, rebellious Rastafarian and give him the opportunity to represent the country. On the other hand I also feel concerned that in the country of my birth my rights are ignored. In this multicultural, multiracial country, its prisons, its courts, even its hospitals don't recognise my religion or cultural heritage. Although I'm not a religious Rastafarian, if I am in prison – at a time when I would need guidance most – I am not allowed religious books, or visits from church elders, I am just not

12

recognised. But the Universal Declaration of Human Rights, Article 18 tells me that I have the right to believe in any religion – or none at all – and that I have the right to practise and teach my religious beliefs. If I can't practise my religion at home, in school or even in prison, where do I go? Must I seek asylum in a foreign country?

Here is a poet who won't stay silent. I live in two places, Britain and the world, and it is my duty to question and explore the state of justice in both of them. When racists express their racism they do not make allowances according to our ethnicity, they do not beat one person harder than another because they have a darker skin. In Britain today many Kosovan refugees are being racially abused and attacked on our streets but they are not being let off lightly because they don't wear saris. This is why when I say 'Black' it means more than skin colour, I include Romany, Iraqi, Indians, Kurds, Palestinians, all those that are treated Black by the united white states. I can hear cries of 'What?' already, but I have to say the suffering I have witnessed means that my conscience allows me to include the battered White woman, the tree dwellers and the Irish; the Irish after all are the largest immigrant group in Britain, and I still remember the notices that said 'No Blacks, No Irish, No dogs'. My Black is profound. I have been in parts of Africa where I have been referred to as 'coloured'; how hurtful that would have been if I simply defined my struggle by the amount of melanin in my skin. In Jamaica we refer to people as brown or red yet we know that we are all Black. More importantly, on my first trip to South Africa just after the official lifting of apartheid, I was surprised to learn how many different groups of White people there were and how divided they were amongst themselves, but then when it came to dealing with Black people they were White people united. The oppressors know how to unite, the oppressed must unite. My 'strong' is the strength that we get when we stand up and get counted as opposed to sitting in 'workshops' and applying for lottery money. When I say *Too Black, Too Strong*, I mean unity is strength, I mean "true" free speech, I mean no justice, no peace. In 1771, 106 ships from Liverpool transported 28,000 slaves "to" Britain, but whilst Britain has tried to retrieve Nazi loot, to bring Nazis to trial, to make the Japanese pay compensation and say sorry etc., it has never dealt with its own legacy of slavery. I would never claim to speak for the African-Caribbean community, I just happen to be one of them, but I want full recognition of how slavery raped, murdered and stigmatised us, and I know a few others that do. Africans around the world are still suffering from slavery today and, one day Britain will have to wake up and face the nightmare it induced. We are not going away.

As I grew up in the Rastafarian community in Birmingham, England, I dreamt of the day when I would be able to leave Britain (Babylon) and return to 'Africa' (Zion), the motherland. Ironically, I now visit the motherland at least twice a year and the truth is that the more I travel, the more I love Britain; and it is because I love the place that I fight for my rights here. If it were simply a case of hating the place and all that it stood for, then I would have left when I first got expelled from school. I want the "project" to work. The day will come when we move from the margins and come to the centre; I just want it to be today.

## Bought and Sold

Smart big awards and prize money
Is killing off black poetry
It's not censors or dictators that are cutting up our art.
The lure of meeting royalty
And touching high society
Is damping creativity and eating at our heart.

The ancestors would turn in graves,
Those poor black folk that once were slaves would wonder
How our souls were sold
And check our strategies.
The empire strikes back and waves,
Tamed warriors bow on parades,
When they have done what they've been told
They get their OBEs.

Don't take my word, go check the verse
Cause every laureate gets worse,
A family that you cannot fault as muse will mess your mind,
And yeah, you may fatten your purse
And surely they will check you first when subjects need to be
        amused
With paid-for prose and rhymes.

Take your prize, now write more,
Faster,
Fuck the truth
Now you're an actor do not fault your benefactor,
Write, publish and review,
You look like a dreadlocks Rasta,
You look like a ghetto blaster,
But you can't diss your paymaster
And bite the hand that feeds you.

What happened to the verse of fire
Cursing cool the empire?
What happened to the soul rebel that Marley had in mind,
This bloodstained, stolen empire rewards you and you conspire
(Yes Marley said that time will tell)
Now look they've gone and joined.

We keep getting this beating,
It's bad history repeating,
It reminds me of those capitalists that say
'Look you have a choice'.
It's sick and self-defeating if our dispossessed keep weeping
And we give these awards meaning
But we end up with no voice.

## What If


If you can keep your money when governments about you
Are losing theirs and blaming it on you,
If you can trust your neighbour when they trust not you
And they be very nosy too;
If you can await the warm delights of summer
Then summer comes and goes with sun not seen,
And pay so much for drinking water
Knowing that the water is unclean.

If you seek peace in times of war creation,
And you can see that oil merchants are to blame,
If you can meet a pimp or politician,
And treat those two impostors just the same;
If you cannot bear dis-united nations
And you think dis new world order is a trick,
If you've ever tried to build good race relations,
And watch bad policing mess your work up quick.

If you can make one heap of all your savings
And risk buying a small house and a plot,
Then sit back and watch the economy inflating
Then have to deal with the negative equity you've got;
If you can force your mind and body to continue
When all the social services have gone,
If you struggle on when there is nothing in you,
Except the knowledge that justice cannot be wrong.

If you can speak the truth to common people
Or walk with Kings and Queens and live no lie,
If you can see how power can be evil
And know that every censor is a spy;
If you can fill an unforgiving lifetime
With years of working hard to make ends meet,
You may not be wealthy but I am sure you will find
That you can hold your head high as you walk the streets.

# Breakfast in East Timor

Ana Pereira is chewing bloodstained oats
In a home-made home in East Timor.
This morning she woke up to a shower
Of bloodstained rain and the smell of common death.
She prayed uncontrollably to a European version of Jesus
Christ, then she went to visit her sister's grave.

She visits her sister's grave every day.

As she was returning home she purchased
An Indonesian newspaper, conceived and printed
In Jakarta. Now at her breakfast table
She is trying to understand why her occupiers
Are so interested in the British royal family,
The politics of the European community
And the peace talks in Northern Ireland.
She just can't understand why the British royal family
Are not interested in the grave of her sister
Or why Europe is so concerned with money.
She wonders what makes new British Labour so proud
Of its women and a thing called an ethical foreign policy.

Ana Pereira has the hands of a man,
Her ears can recognise the sound
Of a loaded Hawk fighter-plane as she sleeps
And her feet are designed to dodge bullets.
You can see her killers in her eyes
And an ever present vigilance in her step.
She has carried all her sisters' coffins
On her reinforced shoulders,
She waved all her brothers goodbye
When they graduated to the rank of militants
And her distinguished stubbornness envies them,
She too wants to be in the hills.

She wants to know where her father is,
She hates bloodstained oats,
And she would love to visit Europe
To see for herself.
For now she will keep remembering,
Negotiating days
Leaving nothing to chance,
Nothing for the Indonesians
And nothing for nothing.

Today's breakfast tastes like yesterday's
And today, the death business continues.
Tomorrow she wants so much to be alive.

## What Stephen Lawrence Has Taught Us

We know who the killers are,
We have watched them strut before us
As proud as sick Mussolinis.
We have watched them strut before us
Compassionless and arrogant,
They paraded before us,
Like angels of death
Protected by the law.

It is now an open secret
Black people do not have
Chips on their shoulders,
They just have injustice on their backs
And justice on their minds,
And now we know that the road to liberty
Is as long as the road from slavery.

The death of Stephen Lawrence
Has taught us to love each other
And never to take the tedious task
Of waiting for a bus for granted.
Watching his parents watching the cover-up
Begs the question
What are the trading standards here?
Why are we paying for a police force
That will not work for us?

The death of Stephen Lawrence
Has taught us
That we cannot let the illusion of freedom
Endow us with a false sense of security as we walk the streets,
The whole world can now watch
The academics and the super cops
Struggling to define institutionalised racism
As we continue to die in custody

As we continue emptying our pockets on the pavements,
And we continue to ask ourselves
Why is it so official
That black people are so often killed
Without killers?

We are not talking about war or revenge
We are not talking about hypothetics or possibilities,
We are talking about where we are now
We are talking about how we live now
In dis state
Under dis flag (God Save the Queen),
And God save all those black children who want to grow up
And God save all the brothers and sisters
Who like raving,
Because the death of Stephen Lawrence
Has taught us that racism is easy when
You have friends in high places.
And friends in high places
Have no use whatsoever
When they are not your friends.

Dear Mr Condon,
Pop out of Teletubby land,
And visit reality,
Come to an honest place
And get some advice from your neighbours,
Be enlightened by our community,
Neglect your well-paid ignorance
Because
We know who the killers are.

## To Ricky Reel

I don't know how to say dis Ricky
But things are not getting better.
We are trying to protect each other,
We are shouting loud on demonstrations
On the streets, in the halls,
And in churches, mosques and temples.
We have done non-violent things
In silence
On the streets, in the halls
And in churches, mosques and temples.
I think of you every time I see water gi,
I never saw you fight
But you are a martyr gi,
That river that runs beside my first kiss place
Even that river
Reminds me of you gi.
Now every time I see your mother
I think of womanhood
And every time your mother speaks
I hear her cry,
Things are not getting better Ricky.
The bad news is
Your mother is so special
She is unique and precious,
She shines in a galaxy of women,
She is a tender one and only,
But there are so many mothers like her,
That's the bad news Ricky,
There are more mothers crying.
Things went from bad to worse
And then from worse to dis serious sickness.
I have to be really honest with you Ricky man
I don't know who to trust,
I look at white girls and think
Do they want to dance with me or kill me?

I look at white boys and I wonder
Do they want to play football with me
Or drown me?
I look at policemen and wonder what would happen
If I asked them the time?

There is a crisis here,
I'm in trouble Ricky,
I think of you every time I'm out in the dark,
When I see pictures of Marx, Lenin
Or Gandhi
I wonder what can we do for you,
Every time I look at Malcolm X
Clinging to my bedroom wall
I wonder what means are necessary.

There is a great wickedness here
And it thrives on people who do nothing,
It is planted deep in the souls of the serious sick
I don't know how to say dis,
But things are certainly not getting better,
The pacifists are out,
The militants are out
And we will not be defeated,
But it's hard, very hard.
I keep seeing your face in my self
And every time I see your mother
There is a constant
I love you Ricky
In her eyes.

## To Michael Menser

There must be some light somewhere
There must be a true other,
There must be more than despair
There must be more my brother,
There must be so much unsaid
There must be an informant,
There must be some truth ahead
There must be a judgement.

There must be a little hope
There must be a truth culture,
There must be ways for us to cope
There must be a just future,
There must be somewhere to go
There must be some movement,
There must be much more to know
There must be a judgement.

There must be ears for our appeal
There must be some progress,
There must be a better deal
There must be more than dis mess,
There must be ways, there must be means
There must be some acknowledgement,
There must be honest go-betweens
There must be a judgement.

It may take God, it may take man
It may take lords of fire,
It may take burning Babylon
It may take something higher,
It may take bad rebellious youth
It may take a sane government,
It may take liars with the truth,
But there must be a judgement.

## Having a Word

I have learnt that equality
May not mean freedom,
And freedom
May not mean liberation,
You can vote my friend
And have no democracy.
Being together dear neighbour
May not mean unity,
Your oppressors may give you chances
But no opportunities,
And the state that you are in
May have its state security
Yet you may be stateless
Without protection.

You my friend do not have to follow your leader,
The government does not have to govern you,
I'm telling you Mom, you are greater than the law
If you are just when the law is not.
You see, once you are aware that new Labour
Does not care for the old workers
You may also know that change
May not mean revolution,
Once you realise that old conservatives
Are running out of things to conserve
You may also know that all politicians suck the same.
Babylon must burn,
Burn Babylon, burn.

Politics is like dis,
Life is like dis.
Intelligence may not mean intelligent,
The news may not be new.

From where we are
To be awake
May not mean
To be conscious.

# Reminders

'The peace garden is opposite the War Memorial,'
Said the old soldier.

'We had to fight to make the peace
Back in the good old days.'

'No, the War Memorial is opposite the peace garden,'
Said the old pacifist.

'You've had so many wars to end all wars,
Still millions are dying from the wars you left behind.'

'Look,' said the old soldier.
'You chickens stuck your peace garden
In front of our War Memorial to cause non-violent trouble.
This War Memorial is necessary,
It reminds us that people have died for our country.'

'Look,' said the old pacifist,
'In the beginning was the peace
And the peace was with God
And the peace was God,
This peace garden is unnecessary but
It reminds us that people want to live for our country.'

## Appeal Dismissed

I can see your fearful tears
Before me on your statement,
From where I sit I can see your dark terrorised skin
Shivering and barely holding your self together,
I can see your gaping scars wide open
Begging for compassion,
And in addition to your evidence
Both documentary and oral
I have before me
The encyclopaedia of your oppression,
I have the names and addresses of your demons.

I don't have to see you dance to know your suffering
I don't have to hear you cry to know that you are crying,
I saw your harassers on the news
I saw your house on fire via satellite,
I have no doubt that you are not tolerated by your neighbours.
But let's face it
You are not a dissident,
You are not even a liar,
You are what I would call a credible witness,
But I have no reason to believe that your persecution was official.

You were not raped because of your dark skin
You were not raped because of your gypsy tongue,
You were raped because you are a woman
And rape is one of the things that can happen to
A woman,
So go home.
You have been the victim of an act of depravity
And you may never love again,
Nevertheless you have only been raped
And in the books that I have read
Rape does not constitute torture,
Not within the ordinary meaning of the word,
So go home
And take your exceptional circumstances with you.

## Chant of a Homesick Nigga

There's too much time in dis dark night,
No civilians to hear me wail,
Just ghosts and rats
And there's no light
In dis infernal bloody jail.
I want my Mom
I want my twin
Or any friend that I can kiss,
I know the truth that I live in,
Still I don't want to die like dis.

If I had sword and I had shield
I would defend myself no doubt,
But I am weak
I need a meal or barrister to help me out,
I know my rights
Now tape dis talk
Of course I am downhearted,
Look sucker I can hardly walk
And the interview ain't even started.

You call me nigga, scum and wog
But I won't call you master,
The Home Secretary is not my God,
I trod earth one dread Rasta,
But in dis dumb, unfeeling cell
No decent folk can hear me cry
No God fearers or infidel
Can save me from dis Lex Loci.

There's too much time in dis dark night
And all my ribs are bare and bruised,
I've never dreamt of being white
But I can't bear being abused,
I'm one more nigga on your boot
Dis night you want dis coon to die,
I have not hidden any loot
And you have killed my alibi.

I'm spitting blood,
You're in control,
It's your pleasure to wear me down.
I can't stop thinking
You patrol the streets where folk like me are found,
I do recall how I have seen
Your face in school upon a time
Telling the kids how good you've been
And of the joys of fighting crime.

I'm hanging on for my dear life,
You give me one more injury,
I've just started to feel like
One more Black Death in custody.
I'd love a doctor or a friend
Or any lover I have known,
I see me coming to my end,
Another nigga far from home.

## This Be The Worst

They fuck you up, those lords and priests.
   They really mean to, and they do.
They fill themselves at highbrow feasts
   And only leave the crumbs for you.

But they were fucked up long ago
   By tyrants who wore silly gowns,
Who made up what they didn't know
   And gave the masses hand-me-downs.

The rich give misery to the poor.
   It deepens as they hoard their wealth.
They'll be fucked up for ever more,
   So just start thinking for yourself.

# Time

All the time of the offence I was at home
The day in question no street did I roam
The alleged offence was nothing of my doing
Can innocence be something that needs proving?

I was minding my own business and quite straight
When the wicked one arrested me with hate
In a cell they gave me water and said 'Cheers'
They gave me Judge and Judge gave me two years.

# The Woman Has to Die

There is no photo of her smile
Dis female of Baluchistan,
Since when she was a playful child
She took her orders from a man,
Her free thinking was deemed as sin
Her intellect and will suppressed,
As church and state wallowed deep in
The twisted faith that they professed.

She would have made a lovely bride
But strange love visited her heart,
A strange love from another tribe
He loved her much, him from Kalat,
Ah yes, forbidden love once more
But here the woman has to die,
For here the church and state make sure
Nobody dares to question why.

Her own father employed his son
To shoot his sister as she lay,
And then the father cleaned the gun
Before they both knelt down to pray,
And now the men can rest assured
That madder men will sing their praises,
Now family honour can be restored
As they misquote Koranic phrases.

Damn curse the men and shame on them
Women do not forgive them,
But wish a million deaths to them
These devils are not God's men,
There is no photo of her smile,
To make the evil greater
The only photo of dis child
Was her corpse
In the daily paper.

# Kill Them Before Ramadan

Ramadan is a time for reflection
Contemplation and meditation.
It is a time when the Muslims of Iraq
(Like the Muslims of London)
Give thanks for their existence.
The soul is cleansed by prayer (they say)
And the body by fasting,
Families unite in honour of the family.
The Islamic mind now reaffirms
That there is but one God
And God is great.
So we must (we are told)
Kill them before Ramadan.

In the houses of Baghdad
They are preparing to proclaim
That Allah is eternal
Allah is absolute,
The most bountiful
The cherisher,
So before they have the opportunity
To tell him that he is,
Before the gracious and most merciful is praised
We must be merciless.
Before their Korans open their hearts
Before their hearts are filled with their beliefs
We should do the right thing,
We must
Kill them before Ramadan.

Evacuate the Europeans
Let us pray for us,
As Ramadan and Christmas unite
Let our rulers know that God is on our side,
And God knows we love Christmas.
But someone must be unfortunate enough

To live under a rogue regime,
Someone has to be a threat to humanity,
Someone has to be The Other.
Our modern economy paid for modern soldiers,
Brave and fearless teenagers
Resolute and steadfast from the Projects and the Council Estates,
Fearing no one but the president of the world
And the God who made his sex drive,
We must
Kill them before Ramadan.

Great hypocrites shed your plutonium tears,
Make yourself believe that you regret your actions.
Why should you not believe that
Your great Britain is mighty independent
And that every missile is on target,
And every target is military,
And all those innocent victims
Are not really innocent victims?
Why should you not believe
That the only innocent victims
Are your innocent victims?
Great hypocrites
Tell your children that you are right,
Make sure they have more than enough clean drinking water
Candy at the appropriate times
And do not forget to set the central heating correctly.
Let them enjoy their childhood,
Do not tell them that Iraqi children shit themselves
Every time the President of the United States has an erection.
Let us slide into our tabloid truth
Let us impress the Israelis,
Let us pray to God and ask him to bless our boys,
Let us remember that some Iraqis are Christians,
Let us kill them before Ramadan.

In London and Glasgow
In New York and Boston
Wives wait in agony

Mothers are on edge,
Professors of war studies
And lecturers of modern history all agree,
Saddam is bad
Saddam is bad.
In London and Glasgow
In New York and Boston
Muslims are praying in agony
Muslims are living on the edge,
And the Muslims
And the Christians all agree,
War is bad
War is bad.

The 'Desert Fox' is no longer sly but illogical,
It kills with confidence and no longer requires a UN mandate,
Left in a corner to dry 'The Allies' are an unnecessary
        umbrella now.
As the president is impeached
And bombs are decorated in Kuwait
We must tell our enemy that we know
God created them from a mere clot of congealed blood,
Let us tell them that we too believe in Allah,
We too have stories about Abraham, Jacob, Isaac and the tribes,
We even have Muslim friends
And token Muslim lords and ladies.
Let them know this is our globalisation,
And let them know
Dis is not a war, dis is a bombing,
But we do not want to hurt their holiness
Intrude on their spirituality
Or disrespect their religion
So we must
Kill them before Ramadan.

Oh my God it's Ramadan.

Dear Soldier
Would you like the opportunity to earn some overtime pay?

## The Empire Comes Back

The Black presence in Britain has a very long history yet little is known of it and it has received very little recognition. Many historians believe that travellers from Africa arrived here when most the inhabitants were troglodytes, it is said that on encountering the climate they turned around and went home. There is also tangible evidence that Black people were here with the Romans and that there were large black communities before they were deported by Elizabeth I back in the 16th century.

On Wednesday 21st June 1948 the troop ship SS *Empire Windrush* arrived in Tilbury Dock, England. Many of the passengers on board were ex-servicemen from the Caribbean who had recently fought for Britain during the 2nd Great European war, *aka* World War II. The great wave of post-war migration from the Caribbean to Britain can be said to have begun with the arrival of the *Empire Windrush*. Three weeks after their arrival a young reporter called Peter Fryer wrote an article in a national newspaper that carried the headline 'The men from Jamaica are settling down'. It was an update on the progress being made by the passengers of the ship, but like many of the press reports of the time it overlooked the fact that not all of the passengers on the *Windrush* were Jamaican, and not all were men.

I have been fortunate enough to have become friends with Peter Fryer and when I made it known to him that I had used the title of his article as the title and the reference point for my poem on the *Windrush*, he said that we need as many people as possible keeping the memory of the *Windrush* alive, and that he welcomed a poetic eye on the subject.

The poem started as a commission for an independent television company called Crucial Films who were working on behalf of the BBC. On receiving the first draft of the poem a representative from Crucial Films told me that they thought it was a 'wonderful piece' but they would not be using it because they felt that the last few stanzas of the poem were too 'political' and too 'confrontational'; what they were looking for I was told was 'something a bit more celebrational'. I then sent the poem to Arthur Torrington, the Secretary of the Windrush Foundation to check its accuracy and for general comment, I will not repeat what he wrote in reply, that would sound too much like self-praise, suffice to say that he and the foundation had no problems with the political tone or the attitude of the poem.

# The Men from Jamaica Are Settling Down

From de land of wood an water
Came they to where de air waz cold,
Dem come to work wid bricks an mortar
They heard de streets were paved wid gold,
From de land of fish an ackee
To de land of fish an chips came they,
Touching on a new reality
Where de sky waz white an grey.

Came they to here wid countless dreams
Came they to here wid countless fears,
In dis drama of many themes
Each one of dem were pioneers,
Each one of dem a living witness
Each one of dem truly profound,
A newspaper said people hear dis
The men from Jamaica are settling down.

The men from Jamaica had come wid their music
The men from Jamaica had come wid their vibe
The men from Jamaica had come wid their prophets
To help keep their past an their future alive,
So to de great future they went dedicated
De great mother country waz begging for more,
De prophets had warned it may get complicated
They said dat there waz no equality law.

There waz no ackee an there waz no salt fish
There waz no star apple an no callaoo,
Soon there waz no time to dream, wonder or wish
There waz so much community building to do,
An back in Jamaica they waited for letters
Where there were no letters, rumours were abound,
But de newspaper said it was going to get better
The men from Jamaica are settling down.

They went to de foundries, they went to de factories
They went to de cities these true country folk,
An when they got down to de true nitty gritty
These true country lungs were soon covered wid smoke,
Some dreamt of Jamaica, some dreamt of their wives
Some dreamt of returning to bring something home,
Some prayed to de God, an they asked de God why
The men from Jamaica should struggle alone.

De struggle waz human, de struggle waz being
De struggle waz charting uncharted territory,
De struggle waz opening up an then seeing
De struggle ahead for de community,
De struggle waz knowing de here an de now
An what kind of struggles were now to be found,
Still nobody knew just exactly how
The men from Jamaica were settling down.

Officially four hundred an ninety-two came
On June twenty-one nineteen forty-eight,
But officials were playing a false numbers game
Now it's up to de people to put records straight,
We now know there were more than eight stowaways
An now we know women amongst dem were found,
Still a newspaper said after just a few days
That the men from Jamaica were settling down.

We know that there were other lands represented
An de women survived just as well as de men,
An we know that our history will be re-invented
If we do not write truthfully wid de Black pen,
Consider de struggles that took place before us
Tune into de bygone an try to relate
To the brave folk that came on de *Empire Windrush*
On June twenty one nineteen forty-eight.

Soon there were more ships, an more ships an more ships
Peopled wid colourful Caribbean folk,
Men, women an children were making these trips
Each one of dem carrying ship loads of hope,
From all of de islands they came to dis island
De National Health Service waz so welcoming
An de movietone voice said that things were quite grand
As the men from Jamaica were settling in.

Dis waz de new world, dis waz de white world,
Dis waz de world they had been fighting for,
Dis they were told waz de righteous an free world
Dis waz de reason they had gone to war,
Dis waz de land of de hope an de glory
Dis waz de land of pleasant pastures green,
Dis waz de royal land, dis waz democracy
Where many Jamaicans were proud to be seen.

But it did not take long for de racists an fascists
To show ugly heads as de wicked will do,
Quite soon de arrivants had learnt to resist
An quite soon they were dealing wid subjects taboo,
Blacks in de unions, blacks in de dances
Whites wid black neighbours an black civil rights,
The men from Jamaica were taking no chances
The men from Jamaica were not turning white.

Race riots in Notting Hill Gate said de headline
De cameras were there as de flames burnt about,
De fighters for race were establishing front lines
As de great British welcome just seemed to fall out,
Race riots in Nottingham City an Bristol
Race riots in Cardiff an sweet Camden Town,
De newspapers said it was dreadful an shameful
But the men from Jamaica were settling down.

The men from Jamaica would not die in silence
The men from Jamaica just got radical,
To counter de negative Teddy Boy violence
They created blues dances an carnival,
The men from Jamaica were steadfast an growing
Despite Commonwealth immigration controls,
They learnt a few lessons an soon they were knowing
That there were no streets paved wid silver or gold.

A new generation rose up from these fighters
A new generation wid roots everywhere,
A new generation of buildings an writers
A new generation wid built in No Fear,
They too fought de Nazis, they too put out fires
They too want to broaden their vision an scope,
They too need fresh water for burning desires
The men from Jamaica are so full of hope.

De future is not made of ships anymore
De future is made up of what we can do,
We still haven't got all that freedom galore
An there's all those ambitions that we muss pursue,
De past is a place that is ours for all time
There are many discoveries there to be made,
An if you are happily towing de line
Be aware of de price your ancestors have paid.

Black pioneers came on de *Empire Windrush*
On June twenty-one nineteen forty-eight,
These souls were titanic, these minds were adventurous
They came from de sunshine to participate,
They are de leaders, they are de home makers
They have been upfront since their ship came aground,
But in-between lines you'll still read in de papers
The men from Jamaica are settling down.

# I Neva Shot de Sheriff

'Twaz broad daylight,
Kool breeze waz
Blowing
Going
East, north, south
West.
Me mind waz fine
Relatively speaking,
Me body waz
Present,
An Natty Dread me deputy waz
As always
Chilled.

It happened quick,
Professionally done
We knew exactly wot hit us.

De sheriff shot I an me
An den he shot me deputy.

For a moment we forgot dat we
Represented
Sum criminal statistics
Bout black male violence,
An
Black male sexuality
An
Black male lack of finance

Word on TV is,
'Twaz a precautionary measure,
A softly softly tactic,
Word on de street is,
De city wazn't big enough
Fe all of us.

'Twaz two black males
Gainst four white cops
Wid six work guns
An two cop coconuts.
Blacks wid badges
Blacks wid something to prove
Blacks wid white dreams
Blacks who fear blacks
Blacks who
Nightmare black,
Payrolled blacks
Who want to
Work it from de inside,
See no future on de outside,
Blacks who want to
Represent.

Represent what?
When me, I, and me deputy
Lay on de metropolitan pavement
Didn't hear no black cop saying
I represent yu brother
I feel fe yu brother,
All I heard waz,
'I'm doing ma job
I'm doing ma job.'
When I waz
De coon under suspicion,
De coon under foot,
Didn't hear no black cop saying,
'Dats ma coon brother
I'm a coon too.'
Didn't hear yu crying when

De sheriff shot I an me
An den he shot me deputy.

When I am wounded
I do crazy tings.

As I lay on de metropolitan pavement
I shouted,
'HELP
TAXI
PROSTITUTE
JEHOVAH WITNESS,
ANYBODY.'
Me deputy waz searching for
His driving licence
An talking to Malcolm X.
I'm looking at the stone in front of me
Wondering
If dis be me gravestone.
I had dat ded feeling in me mouth
An dat legless feeling
In me arms.
I saw me red freedom
Gushing out of me.
The universe meant nothing to me then
The church means nothing to me now.
All those joint ventures
Community liaisons party
An all those expensive publicity stunts
Mean bitter nothing.
Cause

De sheriff shot I an me
An den he shot me deputy.

I had
A burst of angry words
I flashed lyrical fire.
I have
Too many ded sisters
Too many ded brothers
Me children dem nervous
An I have too many dying ideals.

I have too many video recordings
Of official apologies
Official denials
An straight forward lies,
I hav too many poems
About not enough truth
An now I hav a bullet.

We don't want to die like dis.

I, me, an me deputy waz
Looking forwards to
Citizenship.
We want to grow up...
We just wanted to grow up,
But maybe we asked for too much.
My mother took me by the scruff of me neck
To a notice painted on our side of town dat reads,
'The authorities are not here
to love you sucker,'
Den she cried a black mother cry.

Times hav changed
Since
Robert Marley shot the sheriff.

De sheriff shot I an me
An den he shot me deputy.

An we are still waiting
For our public enquiry.

# Carnival Days

On days like these we dance to us,
With the drum beat of liberation
Under the close cover of European skies,
We dance like true survivors
We dance to the sounds of our dreams.
In the mirror we see
Rainbow people on the beat,
Everyday carnival folk like we.

Adorned in the colours of life
We let it be known that our costumes
Were not made by miracles,
We are the miracles
(And we are still here).
These giants were made by the fingers you see
(Too many to count)
Carried by these feet that dance
In accordance to the rhythms we weave.
On days like these we dance the moon.

On days like these we dance like freedom,
Like the freedom we carried in our hearts
When the slave driver was with his whip
When his whip was at our backs,
There is no carnival without us
And without carnival there is no us.
The colours of our stories joyful the eyes
And rhythm wise the body moves.

On days like these we dance the sun
We cannot make dis love indoors,
Or be restricted by the idea of a roof,
Dis soul, dis reggae, dis calypso,
Dis sweet one music we make
Is for all of us who work dis land
And cannot be contained by bricks and mortar,
It is we, the beat and the streets.

The passion has to be unleashed,
To rave alone is not today,
Dis is a beautiful madness
Dis is a wonder full place.
So play Mas citizen
Be the immortal bird you want to be
Bring hope and truth and prophecy
Or meet the lover in your mind,
Let us take these colours
Let us take these sounds
And make ourselves a paradise.
On days like these we can.

On days like these the elders say
Astronauts can see us dance
Glittering like precious stones
On dis rocking British cultural crown,
When Rio's eyes upon us gaze
And Africans are proud of us
With heads held high we say we are
The carnival, sweet carnival.

On days like these we dance to us,
On days like these we love ourselves.

## Naked

Dis is me naked. Unclothed, undressed under
    the light of all the Gods that you dare
    imagine, waiting to be touched with as
    many versions of the truth as you
    can conjure up in your turned off
    mind.

Dis is me. Give me your theory, give me
    your opinion, give me your truth, give me
    your big bad holy book, let me know
    exactly what tried and tested faith
    keeps you asleep.

Dis is me, hungry for the priceless forbidden, looking
    for the man who wrote the superhighway code
    so that I can rob his richness.
    He got insurance, he got the state, let me get him.
    I wanna find game show hosts and put
    the bastards on trial. I wanna kill educated ignorance.

Dis is me naked, revolting in front of you, I'm
    not much but I give a damn. Lovers look
    at me, haters look at me as I exhibit
    my love and my fury on dis desperate
    stage.

Dis is me naked. I love being naked.
    I look at my naked self and I know
    that I was made for nakedness. I see
    my neighbours naked, I see booted and
    suited men naked, and women in purdah
    naked, and all the priests and politicians
    who I despise are naked looking
    at the truth, facing reality, having to
    deal with themselves, by themselves. Praise
    the Gods for the black, brown, white, fat,

thin, one-legged, blind, bent and uneven
naked bodies. Praise the female Gods
and the older Gods for the naked body
beautiful.

Dis is me. Not hanging out on Soho Road,
Handsworth, not hanging out on Railton Road,
Brixton, not chilling on Grosvenor Road,
Bristol, not even wheeling and
dealing on the sad streets of
London, west central. Naked I am, fixed
in reality, not looking for a fix,
not pickpocketing in Piccadilly.

I pay tax, they force me to pay for my oppression.

Dis is my mother. She read a poster on a
hot tin street in Jamaica that told her
that Britain loves her. She tuned
into the dream that made me the
naked cop beater that I
am today. I do all dis stuff for my
mother and she cries because I will
not go to church.

Dis is me naked, jealous, passionate, listening
for the naked sound of liberty,
waiting for the militants to arise, pouring
the lubricant sweat into the system
of rebellion.

Dis is me invading the blank page with my
endless aerodynamic pen, driven like
optimistic hope, driven, raging,
desperate, hungry, inspired by the
chit-chat overheard on stinky smoky
buses
turned on by the politics of the kitchen.

Dis is me. Dreadlocks I. Rastafari. Rastafari.
Behold, how good and how pleasant
it is for revolutionaries to dwell together
in the house of the lord. Knowing that
the real God will liberate those who liberate
themselves I shall fear no religion.
Took away the dried up intermediary, got
a direct line to the great ganja
creator. Dis is me, Rastafari, Rastafari,
Dreadlocks I.

Dis is me blowing my lonely black trumpet.

Dis is me mysteriously trying to smile, trying
to convince myself that dis is the
lesser of evils. I stagger from
column to column stealing from its
stolen concrete as I go. 'Fall Babylon,
Fall Babylon and take your bankers
with you,' I chant as I piss on parliament.

Dis is me, standing under understanding,
getting up and over, overstanding the
corruption of our role models. The
lack of courage of our athletes burns me.
The Vegan sex is sweet.

Dis is my music. Loud, deep, Jungle music.
Heavy, roots, Reggae dub stuff.
I rave like a lover, I love like a raver
I know it's only Hip-Hop Rock but I like it,
I'm so proud of it. We rocked the world
with it. We turned on generations
with it, made love and riots with
it, we created the magic
but we still don't own the magic.
Why must we still struggle for our royalty cheque?

Dis is me fatherless, childless. Who do I go to and for what?
Who shall I cry to? Who shall I cry for?
I need babies to recite to
I need babies to recite to me
my life is full of lonely childless eternities
where only poetry gives me life
and nakedness gives me knowledge.
When I cry they want to arrest me, when I'm in
need I'm suspicious, when I cross the road
they ask me why.

Dis is me. I hate dis government as much as I
hated the one before it and I have reason
to believe that I will hate the one to come.
How did these lefties reach dis Tory place?

Dis is me, squeeze me. Let me free me.
I have come to realise that what you can do for me
I can do much better for me.
Let me do for my loved ones what you will not do for them
I want to hold the hands of my loved ones
(Those who have no one to vote for)
and cause a victorious rumble in dis black universe.
I am naked, whispering screams in the church
of the impatient revolutionaries. I may be
vulnerable, I may not have the education of my critics or
the wealth of my arresting officers, but I have
never felt the need to wear a uniform in order
to break laws and I have never felt the need to
eat dead bodies in order to feel like a good human.

## Adultery

We all say we luv honesty
But den wot of de lies we do
Your luv may lie an yet be true,
How honest can you be?

Live wid your joyful misery
An madness dat you can't proclaim
How often can you change your name?
How honest can you be?

Fake common norms an decency
Designed to give you sleepless nights
Torture your soul an dim your lights,
How honest can you be?

You cannot do conformity
You want to luv more equally
But wot of your community,
How honest can you be?

## Going Cheap

A dollar head shouts 'Buy',
A pound head shouts 'Sell',
A shopkeeper's shouting 'Capitalism will eat itself',
A prophet's asking 'When?'

A caring father on the futures market has just condemned
A family on the West Coast of Africa to five years hard labour.
A speculator called that a result.

Now here's a New World order... *Large burger and fries please.*

It's business as usual.
Earthquakes cost money,
Dams damn the needy
And Palestinians don't count.

Now here's a New World order...

One oriental woman
Supermodel skinny
With
Blonde hair
Black girl bottom
Surgically modified nose,
And genetically modified shit.

It's the economy stupid,
It's business as usual.

## Christmas Has Been Shot

Christmas has been shot away this year,
There are too many choppers chopping up the sky
Too many bullets in the air for good tidings,
There will be no Christ and no mass
And darkness has fallen upon the land.
No one shall make a joyful noise unto the Lord
Or serve the Lord with gladness,
No one shall come before his presence with singing,
And Palestinian Christians who want to declare
The name of the Lord in Jerusalem
Or glorify the boy in Bethlehem
Have been told to piss off to Jordan,
Syria or Iraq.

All the saints have been told
To wait for the resumption of peace talks
And the angels of the Lord have been told
To wait until the Americans are ready
Because Zion means something else now,
And yes it was written that the truth shall flow
From the mouths of babe and suckling,
But babes and sucklings beware
The soldiers have orders to kill,
And the spirit of King Herod is alive.
They're not doing Christmas this year,
It has been shot away
'And anyway
Christ is no messiah,' said the soldier
'This is our Promised Land.'

What we see over Bethlehem this year
Is a spineless, skeleton of a Christmas,
A Christmas that has been occupied, strangled
And driven to tears, crying tear gas and burning,
It's a Christmas that has no songs or sermons

Except the song of the bomber;
As loud as dying
As quiet as death.
Welcome to the birthplace of his holiness
Welcome to the humiliation of the natives,
Here even flowers are shot down
If they fly the local flag,
You will not hear the bells of Christmas
And you will not hear the women sing.
'And let me tell you something else,' said the soldier
'No virgin gave birth here – we wouldn't allow it.'

Sorry gentiles
It looks like it's gonna be a cold Christmas,
Ain't no spirit of the Lord moving over the manger
Just a nuclear power
Flying in from Tel Aviv via Washington DC.
The power of the almighty has come for sure
To suck Christmas dry
And to blow Christmas away.
There will be no mercy
And no rejoicing
And no worshipping any little Black Palestinian boy,
And no crosses
And no three wise women or men
And no Arab shepherds,
Because Christmas has been done in
Christmas is coughing and choking
Christmas has been hit by bullets from the west,
So if you want to do Christmas this year
Take a bible,
Sit indoors,
And do your own thing,
Just don't do it in Bethlehem.

## Two Dozen Babylon

Two dozen Babylon dem a follow me
As me driving in me dreadlocks car.
Most days of de week dem bother me
As me driving in me dreadlocks car.
As I'm shopping de cops dem a film me
As me driving in me dreadlocks car.
I just feel dat dem want to discourage me
As me driving in me dreadlocks car.

Two dozen Babylon dem a follow me
As me driving in me dreadlocks car.
If dem could dem would a chain and collar me
As me driving in me dreadlocks car.
I'm told they're so jealous of me
As me driving in me dreadlocks car.
And dem desperately want fe convict me
As me driving in me dreadlocks car.

Two dozen Babylon dem a follow me
As me driving in me dreadlocks car.
I can see dat de beasts want to swallow me
As me driving in me dreadlocks car.
I don't have a ting to relax me
As me driving in me dreadlocks car.
And de same Babylon dem a tax me
As me driving in me dreadlocks car.

## Three Black Males

Three black males get arrested
When they said they seek two whites,
Dis poet said that's expected
For we have no human rights,
We die in their police stations
We do nothing to get caught
We are only in white nations
When we win them gold in sports.

Three black males in the system
So the system just rolls on.
Can you recognise the victims
When the truth is dead and gone,
Can you recognise their anguish
When they beg you time to care
Or do you forget your language
When three black males disappear?

Raphael Rowe is not an angel
And Michael Davis ain't
Let us be straight and factual
Randolph Johnson is no saint,
The Home Office has a God complex
But that office is not great
For it does not recognise subtext
Injustice or mistakes.

Let all poets now bear witness
Let the storyteller tell
Let us deal with dis white business
Dis democracy's not well,
The cops, the judge and jury
Need some helping it does seem
And three black males with a story
Fight
So truth can reign supreme.

## We People Too

I have dreams of summer days
Of running freely on the lawn
I luv a lazy Sunday morn
Like many others do.
I luv my family always
I luv clear water in a stream
Oh yes I cry and yes I dream
We dogs are people too.

And I dear folk am small and great
My friends call me the mighty Bruce
I luv to drink pure orange juice
Like many others do.
I hope you all appreciate
We give you all a helping hand
When me and my friends turn the land
We worms are people too.

When I have time I luv sightseeing
You may not want to see my face
But you and me must share a space
Like many others do.
Please think of me dear human being
It seems that I'm always in need
I have a family to feed
We mice are people too.

They say we're really dangerous
But we too like to feel and touch
And we like music very much
Like many others do.
Most of us are not poisonous
I have a little lovely face
I move around with style and grace
We snakes are people too.

I don't mind if you stand and stare
But know that I have luv no end
And my young ones I will defend
Like many others do.
When you see me in the air
Remember that I know the worth
Of all us who share the earth
We birds are people too.

I need fresh air and exercise
I need to safely cross the road,
I carry such a heavy load
Like many others do.
Don't only judge me by my size
Ask any veterinarian
I'm just a vegetarian
We cows are people too.

Water runs straight off my smooth back
And I hold my head high with pride
I like my children at my side
Like many others do.
I don't care if you're white or black
If you like land or air or sea
I want to see more unity
We ducks are people too.

I think living is so cool
And what I really like the most
Is kiss chase and I luv brown toast
Like many others do.
I hang around in a big skool
I only need a little sleep
I like thinking really deep
We fish are people too.

I luv the cows I love the trees
And I would rather you not smoke
For if you smoke then I would choke
Like many others do.
I beg you do not squash me please
I do not want to cause you harm
I simply want you to stay calm
We flies are people too.

My name is Thomas Tippy Tops
Billy is not my name
I've learnt to live with fame
Like many others do.
I once was on Top of the Pops
On TV I sang loud
My parents were so proud
We goats are people too.

I luv to walk among the fern
I'm thankful for each night and day
I really luv to holiday
Like many others do.
I've read the books and my concern
Is why do we always look bad
My friends don't think I'm raving mad
We wolves are people too.

A lovely garden makes me smile
A good joke makes me croak
One day I want to own a boat
Like many others do.
I'd luv to see the river Nile
I'd luv my own sandcastle
I really want to travel
We frogs are people too.

Please do not call me horrid names
Think of me as a brother
I'm quite nice you'll discover
Like many others do.
If you're my friend then call me James
I'll be your friend forever more
I'll be the one that you adore
We pigs are people too.

We really need dis planet
And we want you to be aware
We just don't have one spare
Not any of us do.

We dogs, we goats
We mice, we snakes
Even we worms
Are really great,
We birds, we cows
We ducks, we frogs
Are just trying to do our jobs
We wolves, we fish
We pigs, we flies
Could really open up your eyes
And all we want to say to you
Is that
We all are people too.

## Anti-Slavery Movements

Some people say
Animal liberators are not
Working in the interest of animals.
But I've never seen liberated animals
Protest by going back to their place
Of captivity.
But then again
I've never heard of any liberated slaves
Begging for more humiliation
Or voting for slavery.

Animals vote with their feet
Or their wings
Or their fins.

# Knowing Me

According to de experts
I'm letting my side down,
Not playing the alienation game,
It seems I am too unfrustrated.
I have refused all counselling
I refuse to appear on daytime television
On night-time documentaries,
I'm not longing and yearning.
I don't have an identity crisis.

As I drive on poetic missions
On roads past midnight
I am regularly stopped by officers of the law
Who ask me to identify myself.
At times like these I always look into the mirror
Point
And politely assure them that
What I see is me.
I don't have an identity crisis.

I have never found the need
To workshop dis matter,
Or sit with fellow poets exorcising ghosts
Whilst searching for soulmates.
I don't wonder what will become of me
If I don't eat reggae food or dance to mango tunes,
Or think of myself as a victim of circumstance.
I'm the dark man, black man
With a brown dad, black man
Mommy is a red skin, black woman,
She don't have an identity crisis.

Being black somewhere else
Is just being black everywhere,
I don't have an identity crisis.
At least once a week I watch television

With my Jamaican hand on my Ethiopian heart
The African heart deep in my Brummie chest,
And I chant, Aston Villa, Aston Villa, Aston Villa,
Believe me I know my stuff.
I am not wandering drunk into the rootless future
Nor am I going back in time to find somewhere to live.
I just don't want to live in a field with my past
Looking at blades of grass that look just like me, near a relic like me
Where the thunder is just like me, talking to someone just like me,
I don't just want to love me and only me; diversity is my pornography,
I want to make politically aware love with the rainbow.
Check dis Workshop Facilitator
Dis is me.
I don't have an identity crisis.

I have reached the stage where I can recognise my shadow.
I'm quite pleased with myself.
When I'm sunbathing in Wales
I can see myself in India
As clearly as I see myself in Mexico.
I have now reached the stage
Where I am sick of people asking me if I feel British or West Indian,
African or Black, Dark and Lonely, Confused or Patriotic.
The thing is I don't feel lost,
I didn't even begin to look for myself until I met a social worker
And a writer looking for a subject
Nor do I write to impress poets.
Dis is not an emergency
I'm as kool as my imagination, I'm care more than your foreign policy.
I don't have an identity crisis.

I don't need an identity crisis to be creative,
I don't need an identity crisis to be oppressed.
I need love warriors and free minds wherever they are,
I need go getters and wide awakers for rising and shining,
I need to know that I can walk into any temple
Rave at any rave
Or get the kind of justice that my folk can see is just.

I am not half a poet shivering in the cold
Waiting for a culture shock to warm my long lost drum rhythm,
I am here and now, I am all that Britain is about
I'm happening as we speak.
Honestly,
I don't have an identity crisis.

## The Race Industry

The coconuts have got the jobs.

The race industry is a growth industry.

We despairing, they careering.

We want more peace they want more police.

The Uncle Toms are getting paid.

The race industry is a growth industry.

We say sisters and brothers don't fear.

They will do anything for the Mayor.

The coconuts have got the jobs.

The race industry is a growth industry.

They're looking for victims and poets to rent.

They represent me without my consent.

The Uncle Toms are getting paid.

The race industry is a growth industry.

In suits they dither in fear of anarchy.

They take our sufferings and earn a salary.

Steal our souls and make their documentaries.

Inform daily on our community.

Without Black suffering they'd have no jobs.

Without our dead they'd have no office.

Without our tears they'd have no drink.

If they stopped sucking we could get justice.

The coconuts are getting paid.

Men, women and Brixton are being betrayed.

## Biko the Greatness

Wickedness tried to kill greatness.
In a corner of South Africa
Where they believed there were
No mothers and fathers
No sisters and brothers
And
Where they believed
One could not hear the cries of another,
Wickedness tried to kill greatness.

Wickedness tried to build a nation
Of white tyrants.
In a corner of the planet
They arrogantly downpressed
They did not overstand
As they suffered the illusion of the God complex,
But these words are not for wickedness.

These words are for greatness,
The greatness that inspired doctors and nurses
To become educated in the art of freedom getting,
The greatness that inspired educators to become liberators
And a nation of children to become great themselves.

South Africans in the valley of the shadow of death
Feared no wickedness
Because greatness was at their side
And greatness was in their hearts,
When the wind of change went south
Greatness was its trustee, guided by truth.

Now we who witnessed the greatness
Sing and dance to his legacy,
We who muse his intelligence
Spread the good news in Reggae, Soul, Marabi
And the theatre of liberation,
Knowing that nobody dies until they're forgotten
We chant Biko today
Biko tomorrow
Biko forever.

Wickedness tried to kill greatness
Now wickedness is dead
And greatness lives
In Islington
As he lives in Cape Town.

## Derry Sunday

If you look carefully
You will see the impression
Of a body in the concrete.
Sometimes I look up from here
And I can still see teenagers
Taking aim.
One Sunday I shouted up to them
I was born here
Just a stones throw from where you are,
And I live here
Just a stones throw from where I am,
Where do you come from?
So Benjamin, you're British are you?
Forget that crap and
Come here my Jamaican friend
Write a poem about me,
Dis is where I died.

I died on the day God rested,
And after I died I found sleeping difficult,
I found a thunder in my voice
I found venom in my tears,
There goes my son
My son goes there
And there I go I said to the man next to me
But he too was dying.
I want to wake up and live Benjamin
But it's so difficult when I have to pass my place of death
Every day.
I saw you on the television once and I said
That's my man,
Write a poem about me Benjamin,
Write a poem about them and us here
Write a poem about that slab of concrete there,
Dis is where I died.

## The One Minutes of Silence

I have stood for so many minutes of silence in my time.
I have stood many one minutes for
Blair Peach,
Colin Roach
And
Akhtar Ali Baig,
And every time I stand for them
The silence kills me.
I have performed on stage for
Alton Manning
Now I stand in silence for
Alton Manning,
One minute at a time, and every minute counts.
When I am standing still in the still silence
I always wonder if there is something
About the deaths of
Marcia Laws
Oscar Okoye
Or
Joy Gardner
That can wake dis sleepy nation.
Are they too hot for cool Britannia?

When I stand in silence for
Michael Menson
Manish Patel
Or
Ricky Reel
I am overwhelmed with honest militancy,
I've listened to the life stories of
Stephen Lawrence
Kenneth Severin
And
Shiji Lapite

And now I hear them crying for all of us,
I hear so much when I stand
For a minute of silence.

The truth is,
Being the person that I am
I would rather shout for hours,
I wanna make a big noise for my sisters,
Mothers and brothers,
I want to bear a million love children
To overrun the culture of cruelty,
I want babies that will live for a lifetime,
I don't want to silence their souls
I don't want them to be seen and not heard,
I want them to be heard
I want them loud and proud.

My athletic feet are tired
Of standing for one minutes of silence for
Christopher Alder,
I should be dancing with him,
Ricky Reel
Stephen Lawrence
And
Brian Douglas
Make silence very difficult for me.
I know they did not go silently,
I know that we have come to dis
Because too many people are staying silent.

The silences are painful,
They make me nervous,
I fear falling over
Or being captured and made a slave
So I will not close my eyes.
I look at the floor for ten seconds
I look to my left for ten seconds
I look to my right for ten seconds,

I spend ten seconds scanning the room
Looking for someone that looks like my mother,
I spend ten seconds looking for spies
And ten seconds are spent looking at the person
Who called the one minute of silence,
And I wonder how do they count their minute?
I always spend the extra seconds
Looking for people I know,
Wondering how long they will live.

I spend hours considering our trials and
Tribulations,
I seem to have spent a lifetime
Thinking about death;
Rolan Adams
Will not leave me.
I've tried to look at dis scientifically
I've tried to look at dis religiously,
But I don't want to limit myself either way.
I've spent so much time standing in silence,
It reminds me of being in trouble
In the headmaster's office,
Waiting for the judgement.
I've spent hours
Standing for minutes
Pondering the meaning of life
The reason for death
And considering my time and space.

# The Drunk on Green Street

Yeah I was throwing stones
When the tanks threw bombs at me
But I did it for the children man
Yeah I did it for the children man

There was a time when I just stopped dancing
And nothing wouldn't rhyme
And nothing wouldn't rhyme
And nothing wouldn't reason

Yeah I was out there fighting
But I didn't wanna die
So I did it for the children
God I did it for the children man

And look the rain is falling
Does dat mean death or food
Give me a single act of friendship
Cause I need friendship in my life
And let's do it for the children man
Do it for the children man

Cause dats the way it is man
Dis planet isn't ours
Let's give it to the children man
Let's give it to the children man

And when they grow up you know the score
It won't belong to them
They'll have to do it for their children man
So let's do it for the children man.

Cause dats the way it is man
Cause dats just the way it is man.

Hey man,
What you looking at?

Winchester Library 3
RENEW ONLINE at www.hants.gov.uk/library or
phone 0300 555 1387

# LOVE YOUR LIBRARY

Customer ID: ******7340

Items borrowed today

Title: Too black, too strong
ID: C00398974997
Due: 14 February 2024

Total items : 1
Account balance: £0.00
17/01/2024 11:02
Items borrowed: 2
Overdue items: 0
Reservations : 0
Reservations for collection: 0

Items that you already have on loan

Title: The Christie affair
ID: C017179118
Due: 13 February 2024

nload the Spydus Mobile App to control your
and reservations from your smartphone.
you for using the Library

## The Ride

We first met on a golden night
As the moon radiated love light
On the dock of the bay.
Somewhere between the real deal and an illusion
We lay unapologetically
Stroking each others lack of responsibility.

'I want to be a poet,'
She said looking over the mountain,
'I want to be a hippy,'
She said checking out me natty dread,
'I want to be political,'
She whispered as she admired my scars,
'I may not look it, but I'm really oppressed,'
She said smiling,
Handing me her welfare book.

The sea lassoed the shore
Time and night hovered towards daylight
And bellyfilled foxes sniffed their way home.
She put the blanket over her head
Farted, and fell asleep.

The next time I saw her
She was trying to find The Goddess of Plenty,
Desperately seeking the freeway
And after me money.
'It's different for women,' she said
'We can use men for their bodies
Men do it to us all the time.'
The next time I saw her
She ran over me with her wheelchair.

# To Do Wid Me

There's a man beating his wife
De woman juss lost her life
Dem called dat domestic strife?
Wot has dat gotta do wid me?

Babies are buried under floors
In a church behind closed doors
I don't know de bloody cause
Wot has dat gotta do wid me?

I've seen all de documentaries
An there's nothing I can do
I've listened to de commentaries
Why should I listen to you?
If I am told to I go vote
If I need more money I strike
If I'm told not to then I won't
I want de best deal out of life

De fit cannot go jogging
Coz there's someone out there mugging
When they should be spreading luving
Wot has dat gotta do wid me?

You an me must juss stand back
Coz they're gonna bomb Iraq
It's a surgical attack so
Wot has dat gotta do wid me?

I juss wanna live my life mate
So juss leave me alone
Why should I fight de state?
When I'm trying to buy my home,
I juss wanna earn my bread guy
An feed my family
You may starve and you may die
But wot has dat gotta do wid me?

Poets are dying in Nigeria
Or forced to leave de area
Multinationals are superior
Wot has dat gotta do wid me?

An in somewherestan I've heard
Dat she can't say a word
An he must grow a beard
Wot has dat gotta do wid me?

Wot has dis gotta do wid me
I'm juss dis guy from Birmingham
An all I want to do is live good in de hood,
It's got nothing to do wid me
I'm juss your average football fan
An hey sum foreign teams are very, very good,
Why should you worry yourself?
You cannot change a single thing
All you gotta do is tek wot you can get,
Why should you worry yourself?
Try hard an you will die trying
Wot can any of us do about Tibet?

I see a million refugees
On twenty million TVs
An I think who de fuck are these?
Wot has dat gotta do wid me?

Hurry up I've got no time
Don't you mess wid wot is mine
Yes I signed de dotted line but
Wot has dat gotta do wid me?

Your school has juss been closed down
Your tax is buying bombs
An although you come from downtown
You don't know where you're coming from,
You don't know wot you are eating
Your food has a terrible taste
An you can be sure dat you are drinking
Sum kinda chemical waste

There's a price upon your head
Even though you're newly wed
A police juss shot you dead
Wot has dat gotta do wid me?

An down in de police station
They are killing de black nation
But dat's normal race relations
Wot has dat gotta do wid me?

Wot has dat gotta do wid
De man upon de corner dat is selling guns
So we can kill each other as we rave,
Or de crackhead who is trying to crack up everyone
Teking all your cash as you become a slave,
Or de mother in de gutter who is begging bread
Where de man dressed in de Gucci hails a cab,
All I am trying to do is praise de Lord it must be said
Wot has dis to do wid anything I've had

A baby in Pakistan
Is making footballs for de man
Or is she an Indian?
Wot has dat gotta do wid me?

There's no propa propaganda
About Malawi or Rwanda
An all dis makes me wonder
Wot has dat gotta do wid me?

I used to go on demonstrations
Now me feet can't tek de pace,
I've tried be a vegan
But there's egg upon me face,
My last stand was de Miners Strike
I did de cop patrol,
Now it's central heating dat I like
An I juss don't need no coal

Indonesia needs more
British arms for East Timor
More western bombs to bomb de poor
Wot has dat gotta do wid me?

An over in Algeria
They say there's another massacre
Isn't dat a part of Africa
Wot has dat gotta do wid me?

An I don't plan to go
To an American death row
There's no compassion there I know but
Wot has dat gotta do wid me?

My God, I can see you have been tortured
An your wife has been drawn an quartered
An your children have been slaughtered
But wot has dat gotta do wid me?

*This rant was created for performance and for a long time
I insisted that it should never be written down or published.
But at my performances I began to receive so many requests
for copies that I have been forced to change my mind.*

## Nu Blue Suede Shoes

No girlfriend
No car
No money guy
But I know who you are.
No silver
No gold
No pension
Fe de time dat I get old.
No e-mail
No mobile phone
I don't know where me father is
And I am all alone.
No satellite
Inna outta space,
A little spirit
So me going back to base.
Me nu hav nu blue suede shoes
But me really want fe rock.

No police force
No gun
I don't think life is funny
Still I'm looking for some fun.
I won't dance wid de government
Dem don't care bout me,
I rave bout peace and luv and stuff like
Sweet theophany.
Me nu hav de truth
Nar tell yu lie
I don't hav de answers
I cry,
Me nu own de high street
Dis is not my club
All I want is just a little
Heavy rub a dub.

Women are for loving,
Baby, baby, baby, baby,
Well watered down Reggae for your chick.

The black woman/man
Don't own their music
Don't own their image
Some of we don't even own we name,
The innovators
The creators
Wanna burn record company HQ down
But they need the money.
So cover
Cover
Cover,
Version
Version
Version,
You may be laughing
Because I'm so poor
And you're so rich,
But I toured Russia before you.
You're drunk on the red, red wine that you stole,
You're the rat in the kitchen, now scavenging in the studio,
It's top of the pops wigger
U.B. robbing we.

# Do Something Illegal

Musical streams of joy
Enchanted ravers come alive
De gleaming, joyful beats employed
Are here to help you to survive,
Let de music cover you wid streetwise stuff
Dat is so good,
To de riddim do be true
An mek luv in de neighbourhood.

Let sweet thoughts within you grow
An let your body celebrate
Letting your body go
As righteous sounds communicate,
When de dub has made you rise
An all of you are real an regal
Move de body riddim wise
An do something illegal.

De beautiful electric drum
Is wired for your pleasure
So as you kinda go an cum
Reveal your happy soul,
Feel free to do all manner of things
To help you ease de pressure
It gets mystical an magical
When you simply lose control.

Do not foul informers' fear
When dub creators operate
An let no imposters rob you
Of de gracious vibes you generate,
You may float like a butterfly
Or fly high as an eagle,
De dread DJ invites you to
Do something illegal.

*A dance lyric originally recorded with music with Swayzak in 1999.*

## Translate


Who will translate
Dis stuff.
Who can decipher
De dread chant
Dat cum fram
De body
An soul
Dubwise?

Wot poet in
Resident,
Wot translator
Wid wot
Embassy,
Wot brilliant
Linguistic mind
Can kick dis,
Dig dis
Bad mudder luvin rap?

Sometimes I wanda
Why I and I
A try so hard fe get
Overstood,
Mek we juss get
Afrocentric,
Dark,
Who in space
Who on eart
Who de hell we writing fa?

Sometimes I wanda
Who will translate
Dis
Fe de inglish?

# The London Breed

I love dis great polluted place
Where pop stars come to live their dreams
Here ravers come for drum and bass
And politicians plan their schemes,
The music of the world is here
Dis city can play any song
They came to here from everywhere
Tis they that made dis city strong.

A world of food displayed on streets
Where all the world can come and dine
On meals that end with bitter sweets
And cultures melt and intertwine,
Two hundred languages give voice
To fifteen thousand changing years
And all religions can rejoice
With exiled souls and pioneers.

I love dis overcrowded place
Where old buildings mark men and time
And new buildings all seem to race
Up to a cloudy dank skyline,
Too many cars mean dire air
Too many guns mean danger
Too many drugs mean be aware
Of strange gifts from a stranger.

It's so cool when the heat is on
And when it's cool it's so wicked
We just keep melting into one
Just like the tribes before us did,
I love dis concrete jungle still
With all its sirens and its speed
The people here united will
Create a kind of London breed.

## Heroes

Wanderers and workers
Sinners and saints
From here they all look human.
We that are set in stone
Know their greatness,
We mere words
Recognise their possibilities,
We can see that they are
All romantics, freedom fighters
And intellectuals.
These streets are full of heroes.

# The Big Bang

I was born where the Beorma people made home,
Handsworth, in Brummagem.
For many of my early years
I thought this town to be a cold suburb
Of Kingston, Jamaica.
My then girlfriend Jasvinder Basra
Thought it to be a cold suburb of Jullunder, India,
And we were both right.
We, in our puppy love innocence
Knew that it was only a matter of time and space,
We Dark Matter grew up holding hands
Listening to Reggae and Bhangra
Eating channa and ackee,
And playing doctors and nurses somewhere in the future.

Handsworth does that to you,
Historic and progressive,
It wakes but never sleeps
Concrete with a heartbeat.
A private space for all its children
That is full of stars and it keeps expanding,
It is where voices from the past speak to us
Every day, lived in voices
Of working class heroes reminding
Us that we are all Brummies,
But me and Jasvinder knew this anyway.

I saw riots in Handworth,
I saw revolution loitering on the streets
Where money had been thrown down drains
In front of people who were needy,
But I also saw energy laden creators
Bringing hope,
And building sites of new galaxies
In Brummagem, the centre of it all.

This is where I discovered the nature of the universe,
This is where I realised
That The Theory of Everything leaves a lot to be desired,
This is where
The postman taught me that everything needs poetry,
And that it is not gravity that gives us roots
But the things we do to ourselves.
But it was me that said relativity needs to relate,
Space stops everything happening to you,
And in my humble opinion
Faith and tradition will live next to progress
For as long as it takes.

Cosmology?

Well that's all about me and Jasvinder.
It all started with us
In Handsworth in Brummagem,
Where the philosophers of Grove Lane
And the great thinkers of Soho Road
Now recite Alpha and Omega continually.

Astrophysics?

That's about the nature of our celestial bodies
The application of our physical policies
And the intensity of our cultural intercourse,
It's about the way we greet when we meet
And the exploration of possibilities,
And it must be known
That all scientific studies have shown that
Brummies are at home with new horizons
And a multi-layered concept of place.

Time?
Space?

Time invented itself to stop everything
Happening at once.
Space was grateful
It had been given room to manoeuvre.
They remain good friends.

# Work available by Benjamin Zephaniah

POETRY

*City Psalms* (Bloodaxe Books, 1992)
*Out of the Night* (Gloucester: New Clarion Press, 1994)
  [co-editor: writings from Death Row]
*opa Propaganda* (Bloodaxe Books, 1996)
*e Little Book of Vegan Poems* (AK Press, 2001)
*o Black, Too Strong* (Bloodaxe Books, 2001)

POETRY FOR CHILDREN & TEENAGERS

*Talking Turkeys* (Puffin/Penguin, 1994)
*Funky Chickens* (Puffin/Penguin, 1996)
*Wicked World* (Puffin/Penguin, 2001)

NOVELS

*Face* (Bloomsbury, 1999)
*Refugee Boy* (Bloomsbury, 2001)

PROSE

*Rasta Time in Palestine* (Liverpool: Shakti, 1990)

MUSICAL RECORDINGS

*Dub Ranting* (EP: Radical Wallpaper, 1982)
*Rasta* (LP: Upright Records, 1983)
*Big Boys Don't Make Girls Cry* (single: Upright Records, 1984)
*Free South Africa* (single: Upright Records, 1986)
*Us an Dem* (LP: Mango/Island, 1990)
*Crisis* (single: Workers Playtime, 1992)
*Back to Roots* (LP: Acid Jazz, 1995)
*Belly of de Beast* (LP: Ariwa, 1996)
Back to Base (EP: MPR, 1999)

SPOKEN WORD CASSETTES

*Overstanding* (Benjamin Zephaniah Associates, 1992)
*Adult Fun for Kids* (Benjamin Zephaniah Associates, 1994)
*Reggae Head* (57 Productions, 1997: also CD)
*Funky Turkeys* (ABM, 1999)
*Wicked World* (Puffin/Penguin, 2001)
*The Poetry Quartets: 9* (British Council/Bloodaxe Books, 2002)
  [with Ian Duhig, Anne Rouse & Matthew Sweeney]

This book is due for return on or before the last date shown
above: it may, subject to the book not being reserved by
another reader, be renewed by personal application, post, or
telephone, quoting this date and details of the book.

## HAMPSHIRE COUNTY COUNCIL
### County Library

 100%
recycled paper